Transforming Values

A new way to disciple

Laurence Singlehurst

Transforming Values

Published by:

Cell UK Ministries, Highfield Oval, Harpenden, Herts. AL5 4BX
Registered Charity No. 1088578

Printed by Hemel Copy Print Ltd
Cover design by Simon Sworn
Photo: © Lampoon House

First edition 2010
Reprinted 2011, 2012

ISBN: 978-1-902144-43-6   E&OE

Contents

Foreword

For the last few years I have worked closely with Laurence Singlehurst on a project called Hope Together, I have found him to be a fascinating, fun filled, wise and slightly eccentric Jesus follower.

Through this project along with many others we've been able to play a small part in helping the Church in the UK become much more missional. Nowadays you really do have to be quite an out of touch Christian leader not to be thinking in terms of community engagement and reaching out consistently beyond the four walls of your Church and thousands of individual Christians up and down the Country are catching the bug for sharing the Gospel in words and actions. It really is a good time to be alive as we watch a cultural change taking place in the way the Church does mission.

Could it be though, that a similar quiet revolution needs to take place in the way we now disciple people and encourage them to become fruitful, transformed people ready to play their part in transforming our nation? This is the nettle that Laurence chooses to grasp in this fascinating little book.

I'm going to make sure it is required reading for all our team leaders who still, in this good time to be alive, find it quite easy to get scores on the doors in terms of "decisions" for Christ yet an all together different ballgame making 21st Century authentic followers of Jesus who catch and carry His wonderful values out into a hurting world.

Andy Hawthorne
The Message Trust

Acknowledgements

In writing this book on values, I want to acknowledge the influence of the late Tom Marshall, a wonderful New Zealand church leader who I had the privilege of listening to many times. His teaching on the renewed mind was the first time I'd thought about how what we think affects our behaviour.

The other two people who I've heard speak on the power of values over the years are Dr Randall Neighbour and Loren Cunningham. Over the years these two forward thinking men have both said that if you want to change people's behaviour you need to look at the values and belief systems that underlie that. They have both been a fantastic inspiration.

Also, as always – many thanks to Ila Howard who typed the manuscript, Andrew Wooding who takes my writings and turns them into much better English and the Cell UK team who have made this version possible.

About the author

Laurence Singlehurst

A regular speaker at major events, such as Spring Harvest, and cell conferences worldwide, Laurence has also worked with numerous churches in the UK. However, his particular passion is equipping churches to reach their communities, with an emphasis on network evangelism, which is empowered by cell church structures.

Introduction

I started this book a number of years ago when I began to realise that telling people what to do in terms of discipleship and just giving out rules, was less and less effective. We live in a society which no longer has a Christian moral foundation; the Christian values that once held our society together are no longer as clear as they once were.

This book seeks to bring values to the forefront and whether you are reading this book as a leader or just as part of your own spiritual development, I believe that it contains simple ideas. The challenge is for us to change our values and what we believe as we seek to disciple and grow spiritually in today's world. This book for me was putting together all that I had learnt over many years of teaching and helping people to grow.

I trust you find it enjoyable and helpful in your own spiritual journey and an inspiration as you have opportunities to influence others.

Laurence

1

Truth and the
post-modern dilemma

M odern discipleship—and by modern, I mean discipleship as it has been practised over the last 100 years—has traditionally worked from the basis of law, or 'the imperative mode'. Even though the list of Ten Commandments isn't necessarily used, modern discipleship has that echo to it. In one way or another, people are being told to: love their wives; love their husbands; love God; don't steal; don't have sex before marriage; don't read pornography; don't be proud. Disciplers have encouraged the discipled to: seek the welfare of others; love the lost; go to church; be a part of a small group; reach out in discipleship.

The Christian's life is soon filled with all sorts of things that he or she learns they are to do, or not to do. In other words, modern discipleship methods are aimed at people's wills, through teaching, through one-to-one meetings, or in whatever way the discipleship takes place. Disciplers seek to change people. They are challenging people's wills and their choices.

You will have heard many teachings over the years based on Acts 3:19: 'Repent, then, and turn to God. . .'. 'Repent' is the favourite word of the person doing the discipling. You may have heard that this word means turning 180 degrees, or choosing to be different. But actually, most times when this little Greek word is used, it means: to change the mind or change the way of thinking.

While we in the church aim our discipleship at people's wills, it is interesting that modern psychologists look at things a little differently. They too are very interested in people changing and in making helpful decisions. But they recognise that firstly they must help people with their belief system. What do they really believe? What are the values that they take from their belief system? In the end, it is people's belief systems and the values that are drawn from them that shape their behaviour and their choices.

Imperative-based discipleship made some level of sense for most of this century. This was because, in the so-called Christian countries, many people consciously and subconsciously believed in Christian values, and these values and their Christian understanding had shaped their basis of right and wrong. Yes, we have been living in a time of modernity, with science, technology and mankind trying to make a better, if not perfect, world. But modernity, as it was shaped from the 1870s onwards, embraced Christian morality as its foundation, even though it was not embracing a purely Christian view and promoting God.

So imagine with me that you have gone back in time and had a conversation with your grandmother, who may never have gone to church. The conversation may go a little bit like this. 'Granny, tell me about sex. Is this something I can do whenever I want with whomever I want, and in whatever way catches my fancy?' Your grandmother would in all probability reply, 'Certainly not!' Or if she was an enlightened grandmother, she may say: 'Sex is a wonderful thing, but it's best kept within the confines of marriage.'

This imaginary conversation then proceeds to the next few questions: 'Now, Granny, tell me about marriage. Can I just ignore it and have as many relationships as I want? A few years here and a few years there? And does it really matter if kids have parents with stable relationships?' Most likely, your grandmother would reply: 'One partner for life is the ideal. And the best thing for children is a mother and a father in a long-term relationship.' If you asked your grandmother: 'What makes a relationship work? What glues together this marriage you're talking about?' she would probably have answered with words like commitment and sacrifice.

While you're still in the past, you have a quick chat with your grandfather: 'Hey Granddad, tell me what you think about work.' As he answers, he may well talk about vocation. He may express the opinion that some jobs are sacrificial in their nature and worth doing—like being a teacher, a nurse, a fireman—because in the end it doesn't matter what you're paid, it is the joy of serving. He also might talk about honesty and integrity, and hard work and loyalty.

Individuals who came to Christian faith in the last 100 years could be discipled using the imperative method. This was because in their hearts and in their minds, they actually knew what Christian values were. They may not actually have been living them, but when the imperatives came, from the church and from Christian disciplers, they made perfect and real sense.

I grew up in the sixties, when rebellion was in the air. Us sixties kids knew there were moral values and guidelines that strongly suggested we weren't meant to take drugs, or to have various sexual relationships. We were also aware that there had always been a minority of people who lived these ways, but we were a generation that were going to make that the lifestyle of everybody. We rebelled with great eagerness. These values of the past made no sense to us. Yet when I became a Christian in the early seventies, I could still just about be discipled by the imperative method, because deep down, these values still had a faint echo in my mind.

Today, the western world is different. Young people are growing up in countries where the rebellious values of the fifties and the sixties are now the norm. The majority of people will be sexually active by the time they are 18. Many will be involved in drugs to some extent. Their values are the values of the TV soaps and dramas. They are shaped by their peers.

Today it makes little sense that imperative-based discipleship is the main tool in the church's armoury. Even though the imperatives may be perfectly correct, and these traditional values may indeed be the way people need to live, they don't understand why. To the current generation, these commands and imperatives don't bring any echo of a forgotten value system. In fact, they are the exact opposite of the way they are currently living.

Our discipleship may look a little like the following diagram. Here you can see young people entering a box. This box is controlled by the peers, by the people who are already in it, with a set of imperatives that are laid down by the authority figures. When new people come into the box, very often their behaviour will have to change to be in line with the peers and the imperatives laid down by the authority figures.

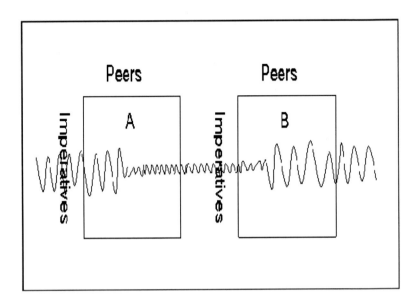

This is indeed how drug rehabilitation centres often work. Most drug rehabs have huge success while people are on the programme. The clients come into a no-drug environment, there are other people on the programme who are drug-free, and there is huge external pressure placed on them to become drug-free too. And they do. In a sense, this is how the church has discipled. Other mature Christians are living in the way they want these new folk to live, and the church leaders state clearly what they believe is right and wrong.

However, when a person leaves a drug rehabilitation centre and goes back into the world they came from, once again they face people who are taking drugs; they are thrown back into the middle of a culture where the imperative is to take drugs. The only people that stay free are the drug addicts who have changed their belief and value systems: they no longer believe the same things about themselves and their world; they have come to terms with something of their past and background; they have placed a different value on themselves; they have a far more positive picture of their worth and value; they think differently about pain and rejection — and with these values they can stand, even though there is pressure all around them to take drugs.

Similarly, churches can create environments which will disciple, but when they are not in church people will find themselves in situations where there are not the same imperatives; there is not the same peer pressure. It could be work; it could be university.

Take John as an example, a Christian boy who has lived his whole life in a positive Christian environment. But he's left home and his local church, and he's now at university. There is a knock on his door one night at 2am. A beautiful young girl comes into his room, wearing a dressing gown. She looks at John, who she hardly knows, and says: 'I'm bored. Do you want some fun?' At that point she loosens her dressing gown and stands there stark naked.

There is no imperative or peer pressure that is going to stop John giving in. The only thing that would stop John taking this extremely generous offer on board—which I am sure he would be very tempted about and flattered to receive—would be a different value system, a value system in which he actually thinks differently about life, himself and what real love is.

John thanks this young lady for her offer and graciously turns her down. John is one of my heroes. This is value-based discipleship.

Now imagine Ian, in a crowded boardroom, a lawyer involved in one of the great business deals of the eighties. The famous chairman at the other end of the table is pushing for the deal to happen, and Ian suddenly realises that something is not quite right. The figures don't add up. He tries to point out that all is not well, but suddenly a huge amount of pressure is applied to him.

It is pointed out to Ian that this company gives a great deal of work to his firm. Everyone in the room, except for Ian who is not that senior, is pushing for the deal. What does he do? Give in? Go with the flow? Well, in this particular case, Ian's values were such that he could not let things go through, so he raised his objections again. This time the chairman exploded, but Ian held his nerve. The fact is, even though Ian thought the figures might be wrong, he didn't believe it was deliberately malicious or deceitful. Nonetheless, the document with the figures was not right.

There was much scurrying round and looking into things, and eventually it was found that Ian was indeed right. A few days later a more reflective chairman of this big company thanked Ian for his courage and apologised for his behaviour. Another hero.

The challenge is this: in our modern world many of us are programmed by the values of the world, which are far from the values of our Christian faith. We have absorbed—via the television and media, or via our peers—a contrasting set of values that offer us another way to live. The church can try to correct people's behaviour by creating imperative environments, but as we have already indicated, most people live the majority of their lives outside the box. It is here that they will be guided by their beliefs and values.

The church must look to changing the programme. It needs to recognise that behind every positive act or way of behaving that it wants to see in people, there are some key beliefs and values.

Our culture is becoming what we call post-modern. In other words, it rejects the sense of a meta-parable—a big story that covers all of life. Post-modernism says that there is no universal truth to live our lives by. In other words, everything is right and nothing is wrong—except of course, saying categorically that you're right, or doing horrid things to little children.

So for a great deal of life, particularly when it comes to personal morality, people are deciding for themselves what is right and wrong. They will perhaps embrace some universal principles (don't steal; don't murder), but, largely speaking, they are conducting their relationships and living their lives as they see fit.

Judith Harris, an American sociologist, looks at this in a slightly different way. In her book, *The Nurture Assumption*, she puts forward the argument that people are not as determined by their heredity and genetics as was previously thought. In her opinion, our social norms mainly come from the culture we are brought up in, the morality of the day. She argues that we are shaped by our peer groups. The values and actions that we perceive in the people we look up to are the ones that shape us.

She believes in a dominant culture, which is the culture of our peers, and a subculture, which is the values of our background, our church, our family. She sees the front door between the two as a turnstile so, for

12

example, when young people are at church, they put aside the values of the peer group, their dominant culture, and pick up the values of the church subculture. This gives them the capacity to live in two worlds at once with very little conscience. So they are not rebelling as we were in the sixties, they are just behaving.

I call this phenomenon 'enthusiastic dualism'. When we were young we did things we should not have and perhaps we still do, but our conscience helped us deal with it. Now we have a generation of people whose level of conscience is much reduced which enables them to move from something they have done wrong, perhaps living in a way that is contrary to their family values and beliefs, arrive at a worship service, put their hands up and be fully involved. When I first began to see this in the early nineties I was amazed.

Of course we do not just see this in young people. It can be seen in adults too albeit in a more sophisticated way usually presenting as materialism and lack of integrity.

Implications

There are massive implications to this which are primarily to do with mission. In our world today the unchurched are no longer convinced by truth alone. In the fifties when people heard Billy Graham speak they understood his words because their Sunday school background had taught them   conscience and morality and they had respect for authority figures both political and spiritual. However, we now live in a different world where, sadly, we have lost a measure of respect for political and spiritual leaders. The voting public give politicians their trust in two areas: one, that they will be told the truth and: two, they will not abuse the privileges they are given. In many countries and in particular in the UK we have had a shock. We have found out, sadly, that it appears the public are not always told the truth and many politicians have not lived in the spirit of the law and have taken advantage. So, today, we are not just convinced by words we want to see underlying reality. Perhaps this has always been true in a pagan world.

Jesus seemed to understand that his message to his disciples and the crowds should be a mixture of words and 'touch and see'. He was not relying just on the power of the spoken word. His example, his demonstration of love and power, ultimately seen in his death and resurrection, showed people that his love was real, his life was real and therefore his words could be trusted—he was authentic and connected to our world. I believe mission needs that today; Jesus sent us into the world to be his disciples, his ambassadors and whenever people hear Christian ideas they will check out the church, the young people to see if they are real.

In the seventies church youth groups grew like mad, not only with Christians but also with many unchurched young people. This was due to two important ingredients. One: young people are by definition connected to their school friends, and two: as Christianity came alive for them they became authentic and a great many unchurched people came to faith. I can remember going to youth groups that had several hundred people in them and all over this country there are churches that grew out of dynamic youth groups. However, today that is not the case and many of these youth groups are very small as we struggle to keep our Christian young people let alone win anyone. So, imagine the following scenario with me.

Unchurched John hears the Christian message and decides to see if what he has understood is true. He will check out the local Christians and I think he will find two groups of Christian young people. Group A go to church but in their leisure time they do exactly the same things as unchurched John. Their lifestyle is no different from his and they are living in two worlds at once, so they are enthusiastically dualistic. Unchurched John thinks, "this cannot be true". Group B are 'authentic' Christian young people who are totally immersed in Christian culture. They don't smell or look like their unchurched peers and, as far as unchurched John is concerned, they come from planet Mars and therefore he concludes that Christianity is really not for him.

So, the challenge for the church in the context of mission is the same for young people and for adults. We should be fully connected to our culture as much as possible and, to coin a phrase, we need to 'smell like them' and 'look like them' but not live like them. We need a measure of authenticity and to allow our Christian values to affect our behaviour and how we live. For example, as a young person we may go out with our friends and if they get drunk we don't—we have different sexual and moral values and we live by those. However, we aim not to take a holier than thou or better than thou stance because we want to love people. As an adult in our workplace and in life we want to live by the values that I outline in this booklet.

The end result of all this is that telling people what to do, giving them 'Christian' rules, outlining expected behaviour—whether its about sex, how they treat people, their money, their relationships or about reading the Bible and praying—is not going to work as it once did because they don't have the corresponding values that relate to these behaviours.

This is illustrated for us very well in the New Testament as the disciples struggled with the same issues in a Roman pagan environment. James 1:8 talks about a '. . . *double-minded man, unstable in all he does.*'

What we are now trying to do is to understand that to create stability and real discipleship we have to renew people's thinking and value systems. Romans 12:2 puts it this way *'do not be conformed by this world but be transformed by the renewing of your mind, then you will prove what is the will of God.'* So it is the change of people's inner belief and value systems that is essential when we are strongly influenced by a pagan or worldly value system.

James Featherby, a lawyer friend, summarises the importance of values with this quote *'a chosen response based on understanding is more effective than a coerced response based on obedience as this requires habit and reflection. It is the only thing that produces maturity.'*

2

Changing our values

In this book we want to look at change, particularly as it relates to people's value systems. As mentioned in chapter one, one of the key words that signifies change in the New Testament is 'repent'.

Jesus said:

> *'The time has come. The kingdom of God is near. Repent and believe the good news!'* Mark 1:15

Right at the beginning of his ministry, Jesus called on people to repent and believe in the good news of the gospel. To the early followers of Jesus, this word perhaps had a very different connotation to what it might mean to us. Today, the word 'repent' has two major connotations. One concerns the negative things we might do, such as our sins, or entertaining bad thoughts. Secondly, people will say it is about changing direction, making a 180-degree turn. This implies that repentance is aimed at the will and is about making choices.

However, as already mentioned in Chapter 1, this little Greek word means to change one's mind. It is about a way of thinking, a way of seeing. In other words, Jesus was saying to people: 'See the world in a whole new way. See God as he really is. See yourself as he sees you. See people and his creation in a different way.'

Our actions are strongly influenced by our belief and value systems. Therefore, it should not be a surprise to us that Jesus challenges us in the area of our beliefs and values. Of course, as we are called to follow Jesus and walk in dynamic repentance, there are many bad actions in our lives which relate to our negative belief and value systems. Undoubtedly, Jesus is calling us to leave these behind.

It is the argument of this book, however, that many Christians end up in the worst of all worlds. They desperately try to leave behind these negative actions—the things they do that they should not be doing—and in that sense they are repenting. But in another sense, they still have deeply embedded in their hearts and minds a worldly view of life. They have not fully repented and asked themselves: 'Do I believe what Jesus believes about the Father, about me, and about people in the world?' This results in so many Christians being double-minded as James puts it (in James 1:7-8), as well as unstable. One example is wanting to love certain people, yet when looking at them seeing them from a human and worldly viewpoint and struggling.

This theme is taken up by the Apostle Paul in Romans 12:1-2:

> 'Therefore, I urge you, brothers, in view of God's mercy, to offer your bodies as living sacrifices, holy and pleasing to God—this is your spiritual act of worship. Do not conform any longer to the pattern of this world, but be transformed by the renewing of your mind. Then you will be able to test and approve what God's will is —his good, pleasing and perfect will.'

Paul's metaphor is slightly different to Jesus': 'Do conform any longer to the pattern of this world. . .'. The early church was influenced by its pagan value systems. All of these new converts, particularly in Corinth, had grown up in a culture that was full of idols. There was much behaviour that was perfectly acceptable in that culture, but not acceptable when following Jesus. The Corinthian Christians were struggling to such an extent that some were even having sex with their mothers, and Paul was seeking to call them into new patterns of behaviour. But he got to the root of things and put it in a positive light: 'Come on, Corinthians, why don't you see things from God's point of view? Look at his will. It is good, acceptable and perfect.'

In a sense, this dilemma takes us right back to the Garden of Eden. In the garden there were two trees. First, there was the tree of life which symbolised God's perspective—how he thought we should live. It symbolised all that was positive and wonderful. It was about real love. In short, it was about paradise, particularly paradise on earth. Yet there was another tree which contained the knowledge of good and evil. This tree symbolised a value system that mankind makes up for itself. People and not God become the arbiters of what is good and evil. This, of course, is not unfamiliar to us in our post-modern pagan world. Most of our society is rejecting a sense of our historic Christian history, and people are choosing for themselves what is right and wrong, formulating their own belief systems on which to base their lives and actions.

Here is the sadness: as we place ourselves in this dangerous position— as humanity and as individuals—we create for ourselves a very mixed blessing. Historically, we have chosen a few good things. Unfortunately, we have also mixed in a great deal of bad things, and the result is plain for us in our world today. You can see things of great beauty—human beings willing to give sacrificially for one another and who genuinely care—yet at the same time you see those same human beings behaving very selfishly. It was never God's intention that we should be the arbiters of our own belief and value systems. Ultimately, we will be confused and get it wrong. Rather, God wanted us to experience life.

Later in the Old Testament, we see another picture in the Ten Commandments themselves, where once again God was trying to capture our attention regarding how we should live. These commandments are an encapsulation, a synopsis of God's value system, and we see through them a high view of God, a high view of other people and their possessions, and a high view of ourselves.

So, how do we really repent? How do we really change our value systems? This is a particular problem with the church, as we've already pointed out. When a society has become pagan and there is little or no understanding of Christian values and beliefs, discipleship must go back to values and beliefs.

We see this in the early church—through their system of catechism, they were acknowledging that people may have made decisions for Christ as we would put it, but they were not allowed to be full members of the body of Christ until they had gone through a one to three year catechistic

18

period. During this period they were educated in the values and dynamics of Christian living and were offered prayer to break down the strongholds of pagan thinking that they would have developed. At the end of the one to three years, when they were seen to have repented in a deep sense through baptism, then they became full members of the church. This principle is explained in Alan Kreider's book, *The Change of Conversion and the Origin of Christendom.*

The challenge for us today is this: we need to understand that as we preach the gospel and people come to faith, we can be fairly sure that they won't have uniform Christian values. Therefore, when they try to live out their Christian lives—maybe in the context of marriage, as single people, or in their secular workplace—they will end up behaving just like the world around them. They will do business just like everyone else does, and perhaps conduct their marriage in the same way the world around conducts their marriages, because they will not have clearly grasped a new set of beliefs and values to help them make choices in a totally different way. They will also struggle because they will have this symptom of double-mindedness—with a difference and tension between their actions and underlying value systems.

Explanation

So, how are we going to see change? Perhaps the first step is explanation. As members, or even leaders, in the body of Christ, we need to recognise the situation and explain to our friends and congregations the situation that we face. We also need to explain the values and underlying beliefs in a clearer and more dynamic way, letting people experience with God and the Holy Spirit how to work out their parameters.

As an example, let's look at giving. This is always taught as an imperative, and we always seem to be putting people under pressure to give more. But wouldn't it be much better off to look at generosity as a value? Instead of being prescriptive and saying that people's giving must equal 10% of their income, ask people to allow the fullness of the value of generosity to develop in their lives. If we did that, then in all probability what we would see is people giving a lot more than 10%, not because they feel forced to or pressured, but because they want to.

They will have caught a glimpse of a generous God. They will have appreciated that this is part of the very nature of who God is. They will then want to be like him, so they will give. And if they have really caught the value of generosity they will give far more than their money, they will give their time, their energy and their resources.

Reflection

We also want to create reflective opportunities, where we can reflect on our own lives and look at the areas where we know we are not behaving in the way we should. We can reflect on our values and ask ourselves if they are Christian or not. The more we look, the deeper we will go in changing our values.

As a young Christian leader, I found that individuals struggled with me, and my wife struggled in our relationship because I found it very difficult to listen. When this was pointed out to me, it caused a period of reflection. I realised that even though I had already had two or three major experiences in my life that had caused me to have a higher view of people, I still had to go deeper. I needed a deeper understanding of how important people were. As I sought to gain that new perspective and see people in a different light, then I realised that listening was one way I could practically put this value system into action. By listening to people, I was saying to them: 'You are important. You have high value. So I will listen.'

Honesty

Another key to change is honesty. In fact, repentance itself is all about honesty - it is about throwing our hands in the air and saying, 'I don't have it right. I don't think right. I don't live right. Jesus, please change me.' We need to be honest about ourselves. We need to be prepared to come to terms with those areas where our value systems are confused; to humble our minds and say, 'I don't believe all the right things.' Then we can enter a catechistic journey with God, allowing him to teach us his values and to see the world as he sees it.

One way of being honest is seeking to identify the areas in our lives where we still have problems—where we are not free. If you've been a Christian for a while, and you're not free from doing certain things, identify each of your bad actions and ask yourself what values lie behind them. 'What do I need to do differently?' What do I need to believe differently about myself and about the situation?' Ask the Holy Spirit to show you how God sees the situation. Changing your beliefs and values will then make it easier to put into practise the right decisions and behaviour.

It would be helpful to think of this in terms of fruits and roots. We may be aware of some of the bad fruits in our lives. We keep picking them off the tree and they continue to appear because we have not got to the roots. For example, Tom's habit of reading pornography, which he had asked God's forgiveness for many times, was never really dealt with until he changed his value system about women and began to see that they were no longer objects to him but people created in the image of God himself.

An even more challenging spiritual exercise might be to seek an understanding of those areas of our lives which are called blind spots. These are weaknesses which we don't see as weaknesses. They are part of our make-up; we may have grown up with them and therefore we feel these actions are perfectly right and reasonable. When people point them out to us, it may at first appear to us to be absolute nonsense. This is the hardest form of honesty: being prepared to believe what someone else says about us.

Let's go back to my example of not listening to people. It was pointed out to me that I obviously didn't love people because I never listened to them. But this is not how I saw it. I felt that I was a very loving person but I had a blind spot. Yes, I had lots of feelings and emotions of love, but I conveyed to people that I did not care because of not listening to them. I foolishly asked my wife for confirmation of this. Did she think it was true that I didn't listen to people? The look of sheer incredulity on her face told me everything. 'Darling,' she said, 'I've been trying to tell you this for years.' I obviously hadn't listened!

What is the value that needs changing here? Too high a view of your own opinion? Not a high enough view of others? Honesty, indeed, is the doorway and the ongoing pathway to changing our values.

Confession

Another principle to help us in this change process is confession. 1 John 1:9 says that we are to confess our sins. Here, the word 'confess' means to say the same thing that God says. In other words, in confessing we are acknowledging that what God says about our actions is true; we are facing the full reality of how our actions look to God and how they have affected him and his creation.

For many centuries, there has been within church life a sense of general confession. By general, I mean this. We use the words, 'We confess our sins in thought and deed', but we never actually mention what it is we have done. I'm sure that in God's grace we will receive forgiveness when using this type of confession, but we may not learn what is necessary to change the underlying values and beliefs that help to cause our behaviour.

Sometimes we may have gone up to people to say sorry, and they will have asked us: 'What are you sorry for?', making us spell out what our wrongdoing was. Spelling it out achieves two things. It makes us more aware of what we have done, hopefully creating a greater sense that we might want to change. Secondly, the forgiveness is experienced in a greater way and is hopefully more meaningful.

The more that people are specific about their sins, the more they are honest about them and the more they confess to God the greater their sense of forgiveness and therefore the greater their love for God. I think that a generic 'please forgive me all my sins' prayer often robs people of this sense of God's love.

Confession helps us to see our wrongdoing. As we are forgiven, by the grace of God, this creates in us a greater love and appreciation for God. Perhaps you have met some Christians who seem to have a greater passion and love for God than others. It could have something to do with this principle—they love much because they have experienced such powerful forgiveness. This is sometimes true in testimonies we read of people who have been converted from very radical backgrounds—maybe drug addicts or violent criminals—and in coming to Christ they have a powerful experience and powerful love for God, because they are aware of how their actions have caused so much damage.

In contrast, if we live our lives happily committing the sins of pride and arrogance and other sins that those of us who come from Christian backgrounds or a positive upbringing commit so freely and easily—our self-absorption, our ambition and more—because these are never named in depth, we miss out.

It is important that we see the sins of selfishness, pride and ambition are as thoroughly confessed as drunkenness, sexual misdemeanours, or any number of so-called 'bigger sins'. There has been more havoc wreaked across the face of the earth because of pride—personal pride, racial pride, ethnic pride—than probably any other sin. As we confess specifically and not generally, we begin to have a glimpse of how awful these sins are and how wonderful the grace and forgiveness of God is. This not only enables us to love God much more, but it also gives us the energy to begin to change our habit patterns.

Think of sin a little bit like this: chocolate-covered cow dung. It can look fantastic on the outside—four or five square inches of wonderful chocolate—but on the inside it is disgusting. All sin is chocolate-covered. All misdemeanours look attractive for a moment. It is only as we glimpse their true reality that we are spurred to change our minds, and ultimately to change our behaviour.

3

Finding the 4 key values

Having looked at the whole idea of values, we will now begin to look at distinct values that might provide the foundation and bedrock to our behaviour and choices. The obvious questions, then, are: 'What values? And how are we going to identify them?'

In the secular world today, you can buy a multitude of books on values—books that look at values in the business world, or values to bring up children. I am sure these books can be very helpful and beneficial. But some of the values espoused by the various authors and gurus are distinctly humanistic. So let us look at some values that have a Christian basis to them, and to do this, we will look in three distinct areas.

- ◆ Firstly, we will look at the nature and character of God as portrayed through scripture.

- ◆ Secondly, we will look at the Ten Commandments, which are in a sense the synopsis of God's value system. Behind the Ten Commandments lie the character and nature of God. The Ten Commandments are an expression of his character and values turned into laws.

♦ Thirdly, we want to look at the life of Christ. Jesus is our supreme model for living. In him is the fullness of everything. Through the example of his life and his words, we get a picture of the life that we should lead and the values that should lie behind the choices we make.

The nature and character of God in scripture

'He is the Rock, his works are perfect, and all his ways are just.
A faithful God who does no wrong, upright and just is he.'

Deuteronomy 32:4

We see through the eyes of Moses that he understood God to be a solid foundation. Moses said that God is just in all his doings—not capricious, not vengeful, but a faithful God who does no wrong. In other words, Moses declared that God is wonderful, and where we see God acting in judgement, these judgements are in fact an expression of his goodness and his justice. They are not acts of vengeance in a capricious sense, they are not power out of control, but the acts of a loving God who, sadly, has to show us that wrongdoings have consequences, both now and in the long-term future.

The values we want to think about are reflections of who God is. He is just, so justice will be important. He is faithful, so faithfulness in our lives is important. He is generous, so we need to be. He loves people, and we need to do the same.

As mentioned above, the Ten Commandments are in essence an extrapolation of God's character and values. They are not just a human moral code; they are an expression of the very centre of the universe.

'In the beginning [was] God . . .'   Genesis 1:1

This God, who was there at the beginning, is in his essence and nature relational, loving and sacrificial, wanting the very best for everybody. The Ten Commandments, and the sending of God's son, Jesus—who is in himself God—are all a continuation of one thing: at the heart of the universe is some very dynamic morality.

The Ten Commandments

'You shall have no other gods before me.
You shall not make for yourself an idol in the form of anything...
You shall not bow down to them or worship them.
You shall not misuse the name of the Lord your God...
Observe the Sabbath day by keeping it holy...
Honour your father and your mother...
You shall not murder.
You shall not commit adultery.
You shall not steal.
You shall not give false testimony against your neighbour.
You shall not covet your neighbour's wife... or anything that
belongs to your neighbour.'   Deuteronomy 5

The first three commandments are about God himself, that he alone should be worshipped and honoured. From this, we can derive that the first of our key values is a high view of God himself.

God, in and of himself, is holy and wonderful. It is clearly not good enough for people just to adopt some humanist or secular philosophical view. History tells us that the human race cannot easily define morality on its own. Therefore, an authoritative revelation from God himself—as in the Ten Commandments—gives us a fantastic foundation. By having a high view of God, we are dealing with the foundational problem that destroys good values: human selfishness.

Human selfishness will always erode any value system that seeks to put other people first, that thinks of the interest of others above the interest of ourselves. Without God, there is obviously no reason why individuals should not see themselves as supreme. But in the light of God, we are clearly not supreme. We have clearly not walked in the ways God wanted us to walk in, and the most loving thing God can do is show himself to humans in the fullness of who he is: his holiness, his wonder and his love. As we honour him and put him first, our other values make sense. Without submitting ourselves to the wonder of God—and in that sense, bowing our human hearts—we will not come up with a set of values that will be challenging or demanding.

The second key value that is seen in the Ten Commandments is respect for other people: 'You shall not murder; you shall not commit adultery; you shall not steal; you shall not covet.' What this tells us is that we should have a high view of other people. All humans, as well as their possessions, are given massive significance in these commandments. If every human had a high view of other humans, and then out of that value came obedience to these commandments—'You shall not murder; you shall not commit adultery; you shall not steal; you shall not give false testimony against your neighbour'—what a happier world we would be living in.

I don't think I would be exaggerating if I said that more than 90% of the misery that is in the world today comes through the breaking of these commandments. The lying, the stealing, the bitterness, the anger that comes from wanting what other people have—all of this creates a seed-bed for so much human misery. If we all had a high view of other people, what an incredibly different world we would be living in.

Then we have two other commandments that give us slightly different values:

That we are to observe the Sabbath and to keep it holy means that God has a high value of rest and recreation. In other words, he wants us to look after ourselves.

As for the commandment about honouring our father and mother, this speaks to us about the value of authority. The family is the building block of all governmental and authority systems. Later on in scripture we are told to respect governments and those who exercise good government. This, of course, begins with respecting the authority that most of us experience in early life—that of family and parents. I will not make this one of the key values that we draw in this chapter but it is, nonetheless, extraordinarily important that we have a high value of authority, even though at times we may have to respectfully disregard and disobey various authority figures which seek to make us do things that are not helpful or right.

So now we have two key values: a high view of God, and a high view of others.

The life of Christ

*'For Christ's love compels us, because we are convinced that one
died for all. . .'*   2 Corinthians 5:14

Out of this profound verse, we see two extraordinary truths. One is
that the nature of love is sacrificial. The death of Christ on the cross
shows us, as nothing else shows us, how much God loves us. The love of
God the Father is shown in the death of his son. The love of Christ is
shown to us by the tremendous physical pain and depravity of the cross,
and also by the spiritual separation that happened when Jesus took our
selfishness upon himself. From that point on, love had a new definition.
The message of the New Testament is that the very essence of love is
sacrificial. Jesus says: 'Love your enemies and pray for those who
persecute you' (Matthew 5:44). And in Matthew 5:46: 'If you love those
who love you, what reward will you get?' In other words, real love is
costly

The second truth from 2 Corinthians 5:14 is from the words: '[Christ]
died for all'. This statement is a re-valuing of the whole human race. It
puts an axe to the root of the tree of racism, or any kind of racial or
intellectual superiority. It quite simply and powerfully demonstrates that
we are all of equal value in the sight of God. That value is awesome
beyond computation, because it is the value of God's own son Christ
dying for us.

This also speaks of our value as individuals. There are a number of
religions and philosophies where value is derived from being just one part
of a wider community. Sometimes in these philosophies, the individual
seems to have little or no intrinsic value and is therefore expendable. But
Christianity is wonderful in that while it embraces the value of the wider
community—yes, we are a family, and we are all equal—our value is also
individualistic. Each of us has value as an individual, and we cannot just
be sacrificed for the sake of the whole. We are not expendable for the
greater good. We are not expendable for some great ideal.

Jesus encapsulated his understanding of the Ten Commandments in
the following verse:

"'Love the Lord your God with all your heart and with all your soul and with all your mind and with all your strength." The second is this: "Love your neighbour as yourself." There is no commandment greater than these.'   Mark 12:30-31

He highlighted that we should love God, that we should love others, and that we should love ourselves. And he demonstrated the nature of that love, of course, through his own death and resurrection.

In looking at the nature and character of God in scripture, the Ten Commandments and the life of Christ, we have gleaned four key values that should be the foundation of our discipleship. We should use every form of creativity and communication possible to embrace and tell each other about these core concepts, because if we have a glimpse of them, they will shape our behaviour for ever.

The four key values are:

♦   A high view of God
♦   A high view of others
♦   A high view of ourselves
♦   Sacrificial love

The next chapter looks at these in more detail.

29

4

The key values explained

Key Value 1—A high view of God

'Love the Lord your God with all your heart and with all your soul and with all your mind and with all your strength'
Mark 12:30

In looking at values from a Christian perspective, it is not surprising to find that a high view of God is fundamental. In fact, it is the cornerstone to value change. Even if you are a person who does not have active faith but believes in God, you will have a sense that there is some ultimate accountability, that you are not alone just to do your own thing. You will also believe that, in all probability, God has some preferred behaviours. Moving on from this, if you then start to look at God from a Christian point of view, he begins to gain in shape and character.

God as described in the New Testament, and demonstrated by the life of Christ, can be summarised in two words: holy and friendly. He is holy because he has never done anything unloving, he is the embodiment of truth and justice, and there is no darkness or deceit in the nature and purpose of God. He is more pure than words can describe. The Old Testament prophet, Isaiah, when he saw the Lord in a vision, was overwhelmed by his own darkness and selfishness and cried out that he was unclean (Isaiah 6).

Yet God is friendly. The whole purpose of the coming of Christ in the New Testament was to make a pathway for people to have relationship with God—that we can be forgiven for our selfishness, we can surrender our own right to rule our lives and re-engage in friendship with God. The amazing thing about the God of the New Testament is that he wants to walk with us and talk with us, and be intimately involved with the details of our lives.

His offer of salvation is not just an offer of friendship—it is an offer of redeeming friendship. Out of relationship with God we are cleansed and forgiven.

'If we confess our sins, he is faithful and just and will forgive us our sins and purify us from all unrighteousness'   1 John 1:9

We are also restored in measure from the consequences of the selfishness we have committed, and the selfishness other people may have committed against us.

To know you are loved by God and have value means that whatever background you come from, whatever abuse you may have suffered, however life may have treated you, this high view of God begins to dispel all of that. Out of heaven, through Christ, comes an amazing message: 'You are loved by God. You are his son or daughter.' All you have to do is respond and agree that it is true and suddenly you are not alone. Even those who have been most abused have dignity, have purpose. The woman caught in adultery stood naked and ashamed, the object of men's plotting. But after an encounter with Christ, the naked woman was once again clothed with dignity and respect. A high view of God is transforming.

It also gives an underlying motivation to change, because a high view of God implies that there is truth. Our post-modern society would like to say there is no ultimate truth, only 'my experience; only what I want to be true'. But because God is just, one day there will be judgement. This gives us perspective. Yes, we can choose to live any lifestyle we like, to adhere to any value system we want to—that is the freedom we have as individuals. But if it is true that God is who he says he is in the New

Testament, and there is a day of accountability, the option of living any old way you want is a rather frightening and short-term view.

An even more compelling thought is this: if you believe in a high view of God, that love and truth is his essence, then taking his value systems on board and living in his ways will in the long-term analysis make you happier and make the world a better place. Surely, having a high view of people, and seeking to walk in a pathway of sacrificial love, is better than a low view of people and always 'living for myself', which is surely a pathway to great pain for all.

God's values are not some restrictive, life-crippling, happiness-destroying prescription handed down from on high; they are actually a dignified, life-empowering way to live. His values give dignity to people and to you. If you have more than a passive view of God and follow Christ in your life, then you have the privilege of the power of the Holy Spirit giving you the extra strength and capacity to seek to walk in his ways, and you have the certainty of forgiveness and cleansing when you fail.

In having a high view of God we can see Him as both friendly and holy. In Exodus 33:11 it tells us that Moses spoke face to face with God as a man speaks to his friend. Jesus said 'I no longer call you servants but friends.'

We would ask ourselves on a human level, 'what makes a friend a friend?' One of the answers is—they know our secrets and still love us, they know the real us.

When we have a high view of God as a friend we can then begin to tell Him our secrets. I can hear some of you saying but 'God already knows our secrets because He knows everything' but actually God only knows our secrets in a non-relational way. He wants us to talk to Him truthfully about what is going on in our lives. Now this is never easy because our secrets usually include our temptations, our failures and our hang ups. For example:

I find it hard to love . . . I am being tempted. . . I don't know if you really love me God because of . . . etc.

We see this kind of praying in the psalms—for example Psalm 10 is just a long list of whinge and whining and yet the psalmist, having expressed his pain and his honesty is about to come to a place of truth, 'God you are with me.' So this devotional praying, this sharing with God is like talking to a good friend every day. Your emotions sense the intimacy and will respond positively to the thought of talking to your friend God. So our quiet time with God is no longer a duty we feel we must do—we now want to spend time with our friend God, the change of value has changed our behaviour.

Key Value 2—A high view of others

In my 25 years of Christian leadership and counselling, I have found time and time again that the problems people are facing - whether in families, relationships or marriages – stem from the fact that they have too low a view of other people and often too high a view of themselves. Therefore, they develop all sorts of behaviours and attitudes that are destructive to relationships, destructive to other people, and ultimately destructive to themselves.

How many of us have squirmed inside as we have witnessed a husband or a wife treat their partner in a way that demeans them and brings them down? How often have we seen human arrogance that belittles other people and makes them feel unimportant, all because our view of others is much too low?

Let me illustrate this with the following stories.

The pig demon!

Many years ago a man came to a Christian counsellor and asked for help.

'My wife has a demon,' he said.

'Tell me about this demon,' said the counsellor.

'Well,' the man replied, 'it causes my wife to shout, to throw things at me, and worst of all, she won't have sex with me.'

The counsellor promised to meet with them together as soon as he could. On the chosen day the young man came with his wife, whose body language showed that she was someone in emotional distress. Her eyes were cast down, and her entire demeanour showed her pain and difficulties.

The counsellor asked this lady about herself and how she had fallen in love with her husband. It turned out that she was a very artistic, very intelligent person. She and her husband had had a fantastic romance, and he had shown her great attention and charm. Yet not long after they were married he had begun to put more and more of his energy and effort into his business. He was a very gifted and successful businessman.

Slowly but surely, they spent less time talking intimately. He no longer asked her about the detail of her day, and she became—week by week and month by month—a glorified utility service that cleaned the house, made the food and went to bed with the man. Slowly but surely, her joy was turned to anger.

When the counsellor had listened to both their stories, he turned to the young man and said: 'I've got good news and bad news.'

'What is the good news?' said the man, eager to hear.

The counsellor replied: 'Your wife does not have a demon. But the bad news is that you do. It is called the "I am a pig" demon.'

The man was shocked, to say the least, but the counsellor went on to explain.

'In other words,' he said, 'you have lost sight of who this lady really is. You no longer have the high view of her that you once had, and through your demeanour, your body language, the way you have treated her, she has felt like an object. This is not to excuse her behaviour to you, but here is the challenge. If you take a different view of your wife and see her as made in the image of God—if you see her as precious and wonderful and a gift to you and treat her as such, and have a high view of her that affects your behaviour—you will find that all the problems you are experiencing will, most likely, disappear.'

So the young man began to change his actions. When he came back from work every day, he asked his wife about her day, and he listened. If he wanted to bring guests around, he began to actually phone up and ask if it was all right if 'so and so comes for a meal'. He began to buy her little gifts once again, and he encouraged her in her artistic pursuits. Today, some twenty years later, this man and woman have a wonderful marriage because of a value change.

Shirts

Kevin, a successful business man, gets married and he takes into his marriage his beautiful hand made suits and thirty of the finest shirts that money can buy. For the first thirty days of marriage all is well and Kevin goes to work being waved by his wonderful wife dressed in all his finery. On the thirty first day of marriage Kevin goes to his cupboard and finds

34

there are no shirts. He is a little surprised and calls to his new wife Wendy and asks "Where are my shirts?"

She looks puzzled and says to Kevin "And tell me what happens to your shirts?"

"Well, I take them" he says,

"And then what?" she asks

"Well I drop them on the floor."

And then she suggests "Have you looked on the floor?"

So they go upstairs to the bedroom and Kevin looks again and he sees his thirty shirts kicked under the bed. He says to Wendy "Here are my shirts".

She replies, "Oh, those shirts", and as she points to a small box in the corner of the bedroom she tells Kevin "If you put those shirts in this box called a laundry basket your princess will wash and iron them for you but if you leave them on the floor that is where they will remain, I am not a servant".

As he went to work in suit and vest that day Kevin had learnt the important lesson that Wendy was a princess and if treated with respect all would be well!

My story

I experienced this myself in a different way many years ago. Life will sometimes throw circumstances in our way that show us how deep certain values have ingrained themselves in our lives. These life-defining moments normally start as quite negative experiences. It is generally when life gives us a knock or two that we get the opportunity to understand our own behaviour more. We may even gain an insight into how other people perceive us.

In this particular situation, my name had been put forward to be the national director of Youth With A Mission in England. There was an open discussion by various of the leaders—at which I was present—where it became clear that even though there was an appreciation of my gifts, there was also a strong hesitancy about me in the minds of some of them.

Afterwards, I asked one of those present the reason for his hesitancy. He spoke about what he perceived as my lack of love for people. I wanted to know more, so he admitted it had to do with the fact that I was a poor listener, was easily distracted, answered people's questions before they'd asked them, and so on.

In discussion with others, it was plain that this was a perception that many had about me. You have already read that this was my wife's perception! But, as I have written in the previous chapter, from my perspective I felt that I really did love people—yet I was a poor listener. So I needed to go through a process of change. I considered the value again: Did I have a really high value of people? Was I prepared to really listen? I also had to look at some of my behaviour patterns that had developed over the years out of a low value of other people. These included: answering questions very quickly; poor eye contact; poor listening skills.

Having addressed the value itself, I felt that I could go to God and ask for strength to learn some new behaviour patterns. This I did, and a few years later I was offered the job on an unanimous basis.

What are some aspects of our behaviour that could indicate a low value of other people? I've already mentioned not listening and poor eye contact. For many, it could also include the need to win arguments, or telling stories that build themselves up while bringing other people down. This is much practised on Monday to Friday, 7am to 7pm, in jobs where colleagues constantly put each other down; where bosses protect their position by puffing themselves up and making other people feel bad about themselves. This type of behaviour is obviously destructive to relationships, and is also destructive to us if we are guilty of it, even though we may feel a short-term gain when putting other people down.

Another type of behaviour that is linked to this is practised by people in relationships who have a 'vacuum cleaner' attitude. They are in 'receive' mode—they enter into relationships to get what they can out of them. We can say two things about people in these sorts of relationships. One, they will have a poor self-image and have a desperate need for people to build them up. Secondly, they do not see other people as they ought to.

How do you know how you value somebody? By the way you treat them. Your actions will give you a pretty good idea of your value system.

When we look at the life of Jesus, we can see that through many of his personal interactions with people he was conveying a tremendously high picture of them. For example, the woman caught in adultery was an object to the schemers who sought to win an argument. But Jesus treated her with respect and compassion because to him she had value. Jesus washed the feet of the disciples to convey how important they were. He served them because they had value — they were made in the image of his father, and they were entrusted to him to care for.

Key Value 3—A high view of yourself

In the great summary of the commandments given by Jesus in Mark 12 there is the command to love others as you love yourself. Think of those words: 'love yourself'. Having a high view of ourselves is a very important aspect of our lives; it is an extremely important value to have. I believe that many of the most destructive social problems in the world today are caused by people who have a very low self-image. This is not to excuse some of their behaviour, but nevertheless there is a great deal of violence, anger, alcoholism, drug abuse and sexual addiction that is fuelled by people's low view of themselves.

It does seem that in some cultures there is a greater epidemic of negative self-image than in others. This is particularly true within British culture. Even after people have had a profession of faith and are seeking to walk a Christian pathway, you will find many British Christians who are boxed in and restricted by the negative picture they have of themselves.

A year ago a Christian speaker was talking to a mature group of mission workers, and he asked them how many knew they had a gift. A common reply was that they had an idea that God had asked them to do something, but because of the way they looked at themselves, they had never used that gift or gone in the direction they felt God had spoken to them about. In this mature gathering, where every single person had been through some kind of biblical training, about one-third admitted that they were boxed in by their own view of themselves.

How does this feel for people? Perhaps it is a little bit like this: even though they have a perception that they might have a gift or a calling from God, whenever they reach out their hands (metaphorically speaking) to pick it up, a whisper comes out of a dark place in their soul, saying: 'You can't do that. You're not good enough. Not you. You'll fail. They'll laugh.' The inspiration of the moment is thus killed off by the recurring whispers.

Leading plastic surgeon Dr Maxwell Maltz, who was at the forefront of his profession, noticed that when he did minor facial surgery on women's faces—maybe straightening their noses or removing a blemish—many of the women became more confident and adopted a new positive approach to life. The plastic surgeon was quite surprised by this and he began to experiment. When he assured some women that they were beautiful anyway and didn't need the cosmetic surgery, the fact that he was an authority figure meant that they accepted that view. Even without the surgery, they went through a personality transformation. The plastic surgery had helped people create a positive view of themselves, but this was also true of the people who accepted the words of the surgeon. Dr. Maltz was so amazed by this transformation that he invented what is called Physco-cybernetics, the science of self worth, and today all of the self improvement, self help industry and its ideas go back to the pioneer work that was done by Dr. Maltz.

Now you may ask yourself, if this is true, why is it that the same people who in some settings are held back by their low view, are able to be successful at work? What is it in the workplace that gives them the motivation to live beyond the negative picture of themselves?

Perhaps we can imagine it this way. When we're at work, we're running on two railway lines. One of those railway lines is: if we do well, we get promoted and/or we get more money. The other railway line is: if we don't do well, we are in danger of being made redundant or sacked. So, using the old metaphor, a carrot and a stick is dangled in front of us, giving us power to overcome something of our background.

Obviously, when it comes to your private life, or even your church life, there is not that same carrot and stick. You are, as it were, a volunteer. There are no external forces in church or your private life that will force you to do very much, so you revert to living out of your inner values. If these are negative, they will shape you—and worse than that, for many people, they will drive you. You will be forced to find outside environments that will take away your inner pain.

This is why there are many people who are taking drugs, be they of the narcotic variety or the alcoholic kind. They are trying to dampen the pain, kill the whispers, gain the false courage to be sociable, gain the feeling that they can be liked. Of course, while these drugs may seem to give a temporary solution to the problem, in the long run they create a new problem and don't take away the old one.

In one way or another, people become addicted to whatever it is that eases the pain of their low self-image. There are many addictions that can achieve this effect, whether various sexual addictions or other obsessive behaviours such as overeating. Yes, the addictions may give that temporary sense of the pain going away, but they just create more problems.

So, what is the solution? Simple: to realise that it is not a bad thing to love yourself. The solution is to believe that your life has meaning and purpose; that in every human being there are incredible gifts, aptitudes and wonders. No matter what academic success or failure you have had, no matter what the voices of your past say to you, you are wonderful, you have gifts, you have a part to play in this exciting arena called life.

How do I know that? Well, from a Christian perspective I know that God stepped into human history for you and me; that he is calling us to be his children, his sons and daughters. The New Testament is clear about this. 1 Peter 4:7-11 says that we all have gifts. Romans 12:5 talks about all Christians being a body together—we each have a role and a part to play.

Just as we are saying that we should love ourselves, we are not wanting to encourage people to think of themselves more highly than they ought to—Romans 12:3 says as much. But at the same time neither should we think ourselves more lowly than we are; instead, we should have a sober judgement about ourselves. You have gifts, you have certain strengths, but this does not mean that you are necessarily best at everything, or that you have to be. Perhaps one of the secrets of happiness is not to compare your gift to anyone else's, but just to develop what you have.

In the kingdom of God, we are encouraged to be part of a giving and receiving economy. The New Testament values encourage us to give, to walk in sacrificial love, to value others and to value God—but they also encourage us to receive. If we love ourselves, we will recognise that we have strengths and weaknesses, and it is not a bad thing at all to receive—to allow friends and others to encourage us, to strengthen us, and to express their love to us. It is a whole person who can enter into the economy of giving and receiving.

Dr Gary Sweeten, an American psychologist, rightly encourages us to be strong, because the more strong people there are—and one of the signs of strength is your high view of yourself—the more people there are who will be able to be a source of encouragement and love to others.

Key Value 4—Sacrificial love

If you go into any church and ask the question, 'What is the high point of love as demonstrated in the New Testament?', the answer will be, 'The death of Jesus on the cross.' If you ask what one word in the English language describes what Jesus did on the cross, the word sacrifice will undoubtedly be put forward. In the life and ministry of Jesus, but particularly in his death, we see the living embodiment of what his life was all about: to demonstrate love and to show the world that God the Father and God the Son loved us. In the end, that is demonstrated by his death, the sacrifice of his own life.

When the early Christians responded by becoming followers of Jesus, it would have been plain to them that they were going to take on a new way of life and a new value system. That new way of life was about sacrifice; it was about loving and living in a sacrificial way. This permeated the nature and structure of the early church. As seen in the following excerpt from *Apology* by Aristides.

'Christians bear the divine laws impressed on their hearts and observe them in the hope of a future life. For this reason they do not commit adultery, or fornication; don't bear witness; don't misappropriate the money they have received on deposit; don't crave for what is not due to them; honour father and mother; do good to their neighbour; and when they are appointed judges, judge rightly.

They help those who offend them, making friends of them; do good to their enemies. They don't adore idols; they are kind, good, modest, sincere, they love one another; don't despise widows; protect the orphans; those who have much give without grumbling to those in need. When they meet strangers, they invite them to their homes with joy, for they recognise them as true brothers, not natural but spiritual.

When a poor man dies, if they become aware, they contribute according to their means for his funeral; if they come to know that some people are persecuted or sent to prison or condemned for the sake of Christ's name, they put the alms together and send them to those in need. If they can do it, they try to obtain their release. When a slave or a beggar is in need of help, they fast two or three days and give him the food they had prepared for themselves, because they think that he too should be joyful, as he has been called to be joyful like themselves.

They strictly observe the commandments of the Lord, by living in a saintly and right way, as the Lord God has prescribed to them; they give Him thanks each morning and evening for all food and drink and every other thing.'

They showed real love in action. They fasted from their own food so that others could eat. They gave to believers and non-believers. They treated everybody as brothers and sisters because they had value.

'Whoever finds his life will lose it, and whoever loses his life
for my sake will find it'   Matthew 10:39

As we ponder on what it means to lose our lives as Jesus told us to, it becomes clear that we are to love and live sacrificially. Perhaps one way of defining real love is: doing what is right when we would like to do what is wrong. In other words, real love begins when our feelings run out.

Everyone is capable of loving people they like and feel emotionally attached to. We can all love on good days. But the damage is done on the bad days, when the feelings have gone and someone is winding you up. Your emotions are negative, your patience is gone and you want to respond, emotionally or physically, in a way that would not be loving or kind. So sacrificial love begins when the feelings run out. Jesus told us to love our enemies; this is love in action, that we love beyond our feelings.

We have a picture of Jesus in the garden of Gethsemane, feeling the pain, waiting with his disciples who fell asleep while he prayed, having all sorts of negative emotions about the task that lay before him. That task was to lay his life down, so that the world could see how much he and the father cared and loved, and to make a pathway so that we could experience that love and that relationship with God the Father and God the Son.

As we are called to follow Jesus, we are called to this kind of love. Jesus said:

'By this all men will know that you are my disciples, if you love one another' John 13:35

In the following quote, John Stott, a well known theologian and Christian leader, argues that the world will know what God the Father is like through Jesus the Son, and the world will know what Jesus the Son is like through the sacrificial love that Christians have for one another. This is where we learn to love: in the body of Christ.

> *'It is a fact that God is invisible. Nobody has ever seen him and the very invisibility of God has always constituted a major problem to faith.*
>
> *'In Old Testament days, the Jews were ridiculed by their heathen neighbours. "Where is your God? We can't see him. Come to our temples and we'll show you our gods. They are visible, they have ears and eyes and mouths. But where is your God?" The people of God were embarrassed by those heathen taunts and would reply, "True, your gods have eyes but they can't see, they have mouths but they can't speak. Our God, however, has neither eyes nor mouth but he can both see and speak." (Psalm 115:2-8)*
>
> *'The same problem confronts scientific secularists today. Trained to use the empirical method, they are sceptical of everything which is not amenable to investigation by the five senses. They refuse to believe in what they cannot see. How then has God solved the problem of his own invisibility? The first answer is given in John 1:18 (RSV): "No one has ever seen God; the only Son — he has made him known". Jesus Christ is the visible image of the invisible God (Col 1:15). As he himself said, "he who has seen me, has seen the Father" (John 14:9).*
>
> *'That's wonderful, people may respond—but it was also two millennia ago. Is there no way in which the invisible God makes*

himself visible today? Yes, there is. 1 John 4:12 begins with exactly the same words: "Nobody has ever seen God"—but instead of continuing that only the Son has made him known, it goes on—"If we love one another God dwells in us." It is surely one of the most breathtaking sentences in the New Testament. It declares that the same invisible God, who once made himself visible in Christ, now makes himself visible in Christians—if we love one another. There is no more convincing evidence of the reality of the living God, than the love which animates the Christian community.'[1]

Sadly, our modern culture encourages a value system that puts happiness before goodness and teaches us to be selfish. The value system of being genuinely loving, caring and sacrificial, is not seen as trendy, and yet surely this is something that rings true in all our hearts. Why? Because this is how we want people to love us. Hopefully, we will have experienced this as children, where parents sacrificed and cared for us, however awful we might have been. Similarly, as adults, we will develop friendships and relationships where people care for us even when we are being awkward, difficult and nasty, because they genuinely love us and understand that love is about sacrifice.

We live in a society where community is disappearing. Whether we live in suburbia, or urban high-rise flats, the growing tendency is that people don't know their neighbours. There is no community, whereas once there would have been because these values—particularly the value of sacrificial love—had been adopted by the society at large as something that ought to be a benchmark for behaviour.

How can we see that happen again? The challenge that faces the church is doing what Jesus told us to do: loving people; to love our fellow brothers and sisters in Christ, and to reach out, as the early church did, to all of the people around us. Will we do this all the time? Of course not. Sacrificial love is never easy. But as a value and an aspiration, surely this is something that we should be aiming for. Imagine the different types of behaviour that will flow from this. Sacrificial love becomes a barrier to

---

[1]*Excerpt from 'The visibility of the invisible God' by John Stott, in EG Issue 8, The London Institute for Contemporary Christianity.*

the wrong kind of anger, to violence, to unkindness and it becomes a bridge to the building of relationships, to the establishing of community.

Here are two stories that emphasise the power of sacrificial love.

In sickness and in health

The first story, told by Tony Campolo, is about a friend of his who ran a Christian seminary and was very successful, but his wife was seriously ill and becoming increasingly incapacitated. The man told his colleagues that he would have to resign and look after his wife as she had become so ill. This caused consternation amongst his colleagues, who knew him to be the driving force behind the Christian ministry. So they sought to persuade him to stay, arguing that perhaps his wife could be cared for in some other way. His reply was that he had made his wife a promise 24 years before that in sickness and in health he would look after her. As much as he appreciated his colleagues' encouragement, he had no intention of breaking his word.

Tony Campolo's comment on this was that his friend might not be a happy man because of his decision, but he was a good man. The sadness of our modern society is that we have replaced happiness for goodness, and in the end this is a bad trade-off. Attempting to find happiness, because it relates to the emotions, is like trying to find the Holy Grail. It is here today and gone tomorrow. Goodness, on the other hand, is about decisions and about responsibilities. It is within our own power to do our best to walk down this pathway.

Learning about sacrificial love is, of course, a lifetime's endeavour. There will always be situations that challenge your understanding of sacrificial love. In some of these you will do well, and in others you will surely fail. The failures can often be turning points to help us learn what it really means to love others. They can be opportunities for us to call on God for his gracious help.

Choosing to love

As a young man I had the privilege for a short period of time to be a 'Jesus freak' and live in a little 'Jesus freak' community, called Flemmington, in the slums of Melbourne. My main role in this community was to float around the streets of Melbourne, telling people that Jesus loved them. I was living in a rather unreal, but very exciting, spiritual environment.

However, the leader of the community was a young lady called Lorraine, who would, every day, go to the high-rise flats where we worked. She'd find the dirtiest flat, knock on the door, and offer to clean it. When she had done that, she would knock on the next flat and clean that one too. Lorraine had a first class degree from Monash University but had given herself to caring for others.

One day Lorraine asked whether I would take charge of a group of children she looked after every afternoon. Many of these children were from abused backgrounds and were extremely needy. There was one in particular, who, for whatever sad reason, would often come in soaked in urine, with human excrement in his underwear. The girls had learned that if they cleaned him, his parents would beat him up, so they had to love him as he was. I, of course, knew very little about this. Having been asked to be the leader, Lorraine saw the glint in my eye, because the thought of 'Laurence the leader' was quite appealing to me. But she then said something that I have never forgotten: 'Laurence, if you're the leader, remember that you are in charge of loving.' A good challenge for us all.

So, sure enough, I was looking after this group of children when the little boy came in. After a few moments, he realised that I was in charge and honed in on me like some exocet missile, rushing over for his daily hug. But nothing in my background had prepared me for this moment. I had come from a comfortable middle-class background, where we had a housekeeper who on good days would run my bath and make my breakfast. I'd also been to boarding school. None of that prepared me for the smell and the sheer unattractiveness to me of this little boy. The closer he got, the worse he smelled. To my shame, as he threw out his arms to be picked up, I walked away.

That night the girls, seeing I was a bit low, said to me: 'Laurence, loving is difficult isn't it?'

'Difficult?' I cried. 'It's impossible. How do I do this?'

Lorraine took me to the passage in 2 Corinthians 5:14-16 (about Jesus dying for all) and outlined some simple steps towards learning how to love sacrificially.

Firstly, it is all about Jesus. He has gone before us. He is the example. He has called us to be like him.

Secondly, we will only be controlled by love if we see the value of others. It is about realising that the death of Christ has given every human being equal value; whether rich or poor, whether black or white, we are all of immense value. We need to take this on as a deep philosophical and spiritual truth.

Thirdly, we mustn't look at people from a human point of view; instead, we need to see them with the eyes of faith. This way, we see their potential. We do not look at the externals—whether they be pleasant or unpleasant—but at the God-given value of every human.

Fourthly, we understand that because the nature of love demonstrated by Christ is sacrificial, this will be a pathway we will walk down. It means we are lovers of choice, not a feeling. Jesus did not go to the cross full of happy feelings, as we know from what he went through in the garden of Gethsemane.

So, armed with these practical thoughts, a few weeks later I found myself leading these little afternoon sessions once again. Sure enough, history repeated itself. The little boy rushed to me to be hugged. He was outwardly as awful as he had been the first time, but this time I was able to get a little glimpse of who he really was and I picked him up and hugged him. As I did, I started to cry, because I realised that this may have been the first time in my entire life that I had done anything that was not to please me. It was something that cost me.

This experience changed my life and started me on a journey—which I am still on—of learning what it really means to love.

5

Life values

Having identified some core values in Chapter 3 and 4, we now want to add some more practical out workings of them by looking at one or two other things that Jesus said, particularly in the Beatitudes Matthew 5 and one or two other conversations that Jesus had.

Forgiveness

'But I tell you, Do not resist an evil person. If someone strikes you on the right cheek, turn to him the other also'

Matthew 5:39

In saying this, Jesus was encouraging his disciples to forgive the people who hurt or damaged them. We can see here a life value that is about not holding grudges or resentments, but recognising that where people have maliciously or accidentally hurt us they can be forgiven. This kind of forgiveness is not about feelings; it is about choices and not allowing resentments to build up inside us.

Forgiveness is a very healthy thing. Resentment turns to bitterness, and bitterness feeds anger—and we all know people whose lives are shaped by bitterness and resentment. If we have forgiveness as a life value, we become difficult to hurt, difficult to destroy, and sometimes—

but by no means always—our attitude of forgiveness will have a measurable impact in stemming the behaviour of others.

Generosity

'But when you give to the needy, do not let your left hand
know what your right hand is doing. . .'   Matthew 6:3

If you pause for a moment and think about your life—about who has shaped it, and who has helped you—I am sure you will remember someone who had a life value of generosity, not just in the way they dealt with money, but how they handled their time and their energy. They gave of themselves unstintingly and joyfully.

I have been moved on many occasions by the generosity of individuals. My wife and I, as Christian workers, always had enough for our needs, but we knew that because of the life we had chosen we would have to have a simple lifestyle—which we were more than happy with. But that simple lifestyle was made very rich on countless occasions by the unasked-for generosity of others.

I remember a friend who, unknown to us, had decided that whenever he would buy his children something special—be it a computer, or perhaps the opportunity for some extra-curricular activity—he would offer exactly the same to our family. I particularly remember one occasion around the time that home computers had become all the rage, and my children would look on enviously at their friends who began to have these wonderful machines in their homes. We were very surprised one day when there was a knock on our door and a man delivered a wonderful computer and all the gizmos that went with it. My friend had bought one for his children, so he ensured that one came to our house as well.

Generosity with money, whether it is large sums or small sums, changes situations. Can you imagine what our world would look like if everybody was generous? Yes, we can spend what we need on ourselves, and also spend what we don't need, but don't spend everything—take some and give it away. You might say that this sort of thing is just for the rich and famous, but it is not. Talk to most charities and you will find that what they desperately want is the little from many. It is the little from many that changes the world.

As a director of a large Christian faith mission, I learned an interesting lesson. We prided ourselves in this mission on teaching people within it to give. We created opportunities to give, and sure enough, many gave. I presumed that many of these young people when they left the mission would continue to give to it—to their colleagues that they had worked with. But I was surprised to learn from the person in charge of our fundraising that actually this was not the case.

When we did some research, we found that many people did not give to the individuals they had worked with once they had left, nor to the organisation itself. I began to realise that we had created environments that encouraged giving, but we had not taught the people within those environments the value of generosity. So when the pressure was no longer there, the giving did not take place in the way that it once had.

You may have experienced this when you have turned on your television and been moved by a Christian Aid advert. That external pressure creates the stimulus to give. Perhaps you have seen it in church: the dynamic appeal and the sacrificial giving. This is all well and good, but what about when the environments are not there? What we need is the value of generosity, a value that comes from the very heart of God himself.

We see it in creation, not in one form of plant life, but in a million forms. God so loved the world that he gave. Christ so loved the world that he died. This is about generosity of heart and spirit. But it needs to begin when we have nothing. You may only have a little, but you can learn to be generous with that little, as well as with your time and energy.

The truth is that if you are not generous with the little, in all probability you won't be generous with the much. There is always another toy to buy; another little bit of excitement to add to life—but generosity means that at some point and in some way we put a brake on what we do for ourselves and create a surplus of time, energy and resources that we freely give. When walking in this value of generosity, we will be thankful for what we have and will be inspired by the example of Christ.

There is no doubt that as we take on the value of generosity and allow it to permeate our thinking, we will become, in some small way, history changers and attitude changers.

Faithfulness vs. success

'His master replied, "Well done, good and faithful servant! You have been faithful with a few things; I will put you in charge of many things. Come and share your master's happiness!' "

Matthew 25:21

One of the most destructive values in our present society is the obsession with success. Somehow we have taken on the lie that success is everything—it is the key to happiness; it is the ultimate goal to which we must aspire. The problem with success is that, frankly, it is not attainable or achievable. There will always be someone who is better than you at whatever it may be. There will always be somebody who will have more than what you are aiming for.

Success, rather than building you up, actually destroys. How many men have sold their souls for success and worked their whole lives, every minute, every moment to obtain that elusive seat on the board, that extra office space, that particular badge of 'you've made it', only to be struck down by the consequences, whether they be physical (such as heart attacks or aneurysms) or the emotional heartaches of divorce; of children no longer knowing their parents?

The problem with success is that it compares you with other people; it is measured by outward indicators. A number of years ago, interviews were conducted with ten millionaires. These people had everything they'd ever dreamed of. Yet six of the ten were so pressurised by success that they could not enjoy what they had; they were driven for the elusive 'more'.

The value of success is not only to be seen in the world 'out there'. It creeps into the hearts of many Christians who, when it comes to work, pick up values that are identical to those of their colleagues. Striving for success can also be seen in many who are in Christian ministry.

In my own life, I had a shake-up moment when God showed me that the value of success was foundational in my life. I saw that it was destructive and that God wanted me to think about a faithfulness foundation.

A number of years ago, I was asked to go lead the British contingent of a large evangelistic outreach in Greece, run by Youth With A Mission (YWAM for short). As a 29-year-old, I was full of youthful enthusiasm for this major responsibility. When I arrived at the site where 1,000 YWAMers were to be based, I was warmly welcomed by the senior leader as a colleague in leading this major endeavour.

But I was soon in for a letdown. Not long after the British contingent arrived, I noticed I was no longer being invited to certain leaders' meetings. When I accosted the senior leader and asked him why, he informed me that two other leaders in the British contingent had complained about my being on the senior leadership team. For various reasons, they didn't think I ought to be. It was therefore decided that I would no longer be a leader on the outreach. So, from being a leader over 1,000 people, I eventually found myself leading a small team of three.

To say I was upset is an understatement. My 29-year-old ego was suffering a major trauma, and I was not happy. In a private time of prayer, when I forcibly put the injustice of the situation before the Almighty — wanting to find out whether his thunderbolt system was in operation as I had some possible sites for its use! — I felt the small, quiet voice of God asking me if I wanted to know what the real problem was. In a foolish moment of honesty before God, I said, 'Of course, Lord.'

Suddenly, as if out of nowhere, I saw the situation in a totally different light. I realised that the main reason for my pain and anger was the fact that I did not have position, and position and success were everything to me. This was a re-defining moment of my life. I felt challenged by the Spirit of God that I was to be faithful to my gifts, regardless of whether I was the main leader or no leader at all.

To illustrate this further, I had the privilege many years ago of seeing Billy Graham receiving an award from the Templeton Trust. He was introduced as the greatest and most successful evangelist the world has ever seen. I shall never forget that one of the first things he said was: 'I have never sought to be great or successful. All I have ever tried to do is be faithful to the gift of evangelism that God has given me, and to be as good an evangelist as it is possible to be.'

As he spoke, the humility was almost tangible. It was a very inspiring lesson for me. After all, Scripture says: 'Well done, good and faithful servant!', not: 'Well done, good and successful servant!' (see Matthew 25:21).

Faithfulness is a totally different concept to success. Faithfulness is about identifying your gifts, looking at what God has called you to do, then doing that with all of your heart. The only measure is your self-measure against the gift that you have been given.

God is not wanting us to become some kind of blancmange, sitting round doing nothing. Faithfulness is an energy. It is a driving mechanism - but it doesn't kill like success. It produces at times the same results, but the people who practise it are different.

As a young Christian leader, I encountered a highly successful businessman who had a Rolls Royce with a personal number plate, a fabulous office in Mayfair, and all the trappings of success - yet there was something extraordinarily different about this man. On the one hand, he had members of the royal family as his personal friends, yet on the other there were gypsies in gypsy families who were also his good friends.

He enjoyed the trappings of wealth, but you could tell they had no hold on him. He would have been just as happy without them. It just so happened that he was very good at doing what he did. He had a considerable talent in a particular area of business, and in seeking to be faithful to that talent it had taken him to the top of the tree.

Many years ago I met a young man at Oxford University who was desperately unhappy. He had made an attempt on his life and he came to me for some help. In the midst of our time together, I asked him what he would really like to be. He said, 'Laurence, what I'd love to be is someone who makes furniture.' So I said to him, 'What are you doing at Oxford University studying physics if you want to make furniture?'

He said, 'Laurence, you don't understand. My father is a bank manager.' This told me everything. What he was saying was that he had grown up in a family where value was measured by success — where working with your hands made you working class; and where going to Oxford University and doing something intellectual made you more important and valuable.

One of the sadnesses of our society is that often we measure people based on the professions they choose and their seniority within the companies they serve. We therefore create environments that in many cases drive people to do things they are not gifted to do, and into painful situations where people who have not achieved what the world thinks they should have achieved look down on themselves as failures.

My advice to the young man from Oxford University was to talk to his parents, then go out and be a carpenter. He was on a pathway to destruction, being driven by the spirit of success. The fact was that he was very talented with his hands and could make the most beautiful things, so therefore that was what he needed to do. Faithfulness liberates and sets us free.

Stewardship

'Again, it will be like a man going on a journey, who called his servants and entrusted his property to them. To one he gave five talents of money, to another two talents, and to another one talent, each according to his ability. Then he went on his journey. The man who had received the five talents went at once and put his money to work and gained five more. So also, the one with the two talents gained two more. But the man who had received the one talent went off, dug a hole in the ground and hid his master's money.

'After a long time the master of those servants returned and settled accounts with them. The man who had received the five talents brought the other five. "Master," he said, "you entrusted me with five talents. See, I have gained five more."

'His master replied, "Well done, good and faithful servant! You have been faithful with a few things; I will put you in charge of many things. Come and share your master's happiness!"

'The man with the two talents also came. "Master," he said, "you entrusted me with two talents; see, I have gained two more."

'His master replied, "Well done, good and faithful servant! You have been faithful with a few things; I will put you in charge of many things. Come and share your master's happiness!"

'Then the man who had received the one talent came. "Master," he said, "I knew that you are a hard man, harvesting where you have not sown and gathering where you have not scattered seed.

So I was afraid and went out and hid your talent in the ground. See, here is what belongs to you."

'His master replied, "You wicked, lazy servant! So you knew that I harvest where I have not sown and gather where I have not scattered seed? Well then, you should have put my money on deposit with the bankers, so that when I returned I would have received it back with interest.

'"Take the talent from him and give it to the one who has the ten talents. For everyone who has will be given more, and he will have an abundance. Whoever does not have, even what he has will be taken from him. And throw that worthless servant outside, into the darkness, where there will be weeping and gnashing of teeth"'

Matthew 25:14-30

Think about it: is there a difference between stewardship and ownership? Let us look at two areas of stewardship: the stewardship of the gifts or talents that we have, and the stewardship of our money or possessions.

We'll start with the really important one: being a steward of our gifts and talents. Stewardship in this regard overlaps a great deal with what we've said about faithfulness. It is my firm conviction that everybody has talents, abilities and gifts. No matter what our background, no matter what our ethnicity, inside each of us there is some treasure.

Perhaps the most important and exciting thing we can do for anyone is help them find the gold that is inside them—to identify and develop it. Sadly, so many people grow up in an environment where that is not possible. But some of us are fortunate enough to have had the opportunity to at least think about what it is that what we are really good at and to use it in the context of our lives—maybe at work, or in the community. These talents are as varied as the myriad types of plants, yet it is always thrilling to see people do something that is special to them.

In the Oscar-winning film, *Chariots of Fire*, there is the wonderful moment when Eric Liddle, in conversation with his sister, tells her that when he runs, he feels God's pleasure because this is what he was created to do: 'God made me fast.' It is so sad when we see people who have been limited by others, by circumstances, or sometimes by their own negative self-view, and they have not been able to develop their gifts.

I know a lady who is an excellent artist and could have had a fantastic career in painting, but sadly she grew up in a family where to go to art school was seen as risqué and totally unacceptable. Consequently, she was not allowed to go. Unfortunately, she compounded this by marrying a man who was so threatened by her ability that he forbade her to paint or draw, and if he ever saw her do it he would destroy everything she'd done. It wasn't until the last years of her life, when her husband had died, that she began to explore this talent of hers. What a huge sadness that the world was robbed of a great painter.

What we need to do is enter life with a positive attitude that says: 'God, show me what you have placed inside me, and in a spirit of faithfulness I will seek to develop it, whether it is a skill in business or entrepreneurship, scientific intellectual endeavour, or artistic gifts, practical gifts, caring gifts - whatever it might be.'

If only more of us could see ourselves as encouragers to help people become good stewards of what they have inside them. If you are good with your hands and would make a great bricklayer or plumber, should you feel inferior to a university professor or a bank manager? I think not. Our society has sadly decided that certain gifts are more respectable and more worth rewarding than others. Surely we need to be saying to everybody, no matter what their gift is: 'Go for it. Develop it. Be as faithful as you can.' Let's not for one moment think that our gift makes us better than the person next door, with whatever gift they might have.

Hospitality

The end of all things is near. Therefore be clear minded and self-controlled so that you can pray. Above all, love each other deeply, because love covers over a multitude of sins. Offer hospitality to one another without grumbling. . . If anyone serves, he should do it with the strength God provides, so that in all things God may be praised through Jesus Christ. To him be the glory and the power for ever and ever. Amen. 1 Peter 4:7-11

We see that we are encouraged to be hospitable. Hospitality is one characteristic of leaders and bishops in the New Testament. It is also a theme running through both the Old and New Testaments. As God formed his people, the Jewish nation, he built into their laws and systems the need to be hospitable to strangers.

Hospitality is love in action. It is post-modern evangelism. When we share of what we have, when we inconvenience ourselves, sacrifice our time, energy and possessions, we demonstrate the very nature and character of God. In the story of the Good Samaritan, the Samaritan's hospitality is staggering. He took his time in caring for the man's needs, he gave him his donkey to ride on and he paid the bills at the inn.

Can you imagine the impact on our nation if every Christian embraced the value of hospitality and opened up their lives and homes in a new way? Some of you will have travelled to Eastern Europe, or other areas of the world where there is still a culture of hospitality, and will have been deeply moved when your host has given you the meal they were planning to eat later on that day. You probably felt embarrassed, but also incredibly special. And it probably gave you a fresh sense of hope for humanity, knowing that such wonderful people still exist.

When we are hospitable, we are working on two levels. Yes, we are working on the level of the physical here-and-now by meeting people's practical needs. But we are also working on the level of the spiritual, because we are giving people a sense of hope—we are showing them that the world is not all bad and full of selfishness. Through our hospitality we may earn the right to share the hope that lives inside us. Because of the hope that we have, and the abundance that we will have experienced because of it, whether we have much or little, we will want to share it.

Integrity

'Simply let your "Yes" be "Yes", and your "No", "No"'

Matthew 5:37

Recently, a professor from Johns Hopkins University, while speaking in London was asked: 'What is the greatest threat to our western way of life?' Rather than talk about Al Qaeda and the events of September 11, he answered that without integrity our society is finished.

He discussed the impact of the Enron, Andersen and WorldCom scandals, and his conclusion was that our market economy and way of life is held together by the fact that we can trust people. In an ideal world, if your stockbroker advises you to buy a share, it shouldn't be because he gets a greater bonus through the selling of the share, but rather that he is thinking of your welfare. When large companies like Andersen say accounts are true and accurate, they should be true and accurate. When a chief executive speaks to you about their company, they should be giving you the real picture. Without this, people's confidence is eroded. They will either bury their money or spend it, and the infrastructure of our western economy will slowly crumble if there is not enough money in the system.

Integrity is something that is, once again, in the heart of God and is personified in the life of Jesus. In other words, the life that Jesus lived and the words that he spoke were the same. He did not speak one thing and do another. His words could be trusted, his actions could be trusted, and we can have complete confidence in him.

'Let your "Yes" be "Yes", and your "No", "No"' speaks to us about how we should live our lives – that there should be consistency. Furthermore, the consistency should be based on something solid. For Christians, our integrity is not simply based on our relative understanding of what is right or wrong, but our 'Yes' and our 'No' is aligned as best we know to the principles, standards and values that God has set down.

Integrity is one of those values that is best illustrated by looking at what happens when it is absent. Without integrity we have corruption, lies and deceit, with people taking as much for themselves as they possibly can. Selfishness is uncontrolled and rampant. Sadly, it is always the poor, the weak and oppressed who are the main ones to suffer as integrity disappears from society.

You can visit countries like Sierra Leone, which are potentially extremely wealthy, but because of corruption, the wealth is siphoned off into the lifestyles of the few while the many face hospitals with no electricity, few doctors and extremely poor facilities. The poor live in shanty-towns, where there might be one stand-pipe for 4,000 people, no toilets, and where disease and poverty are widespread.

But of course, we don't have to go to Africa to find corruption or the impact of lack of integrity. We can look at our own society and hear the growing statistics of benefit fraud, smuggling, tax evasion, employee theft, and on it goes - billions of pounds disappearing because of the lack of integrity. This is money that could be spent on our hospitals and schools, or given away to needy nations.

We could also look at the perceived loss of integrity in our political systems. Sometimes politicians seem amazed that young people are somewhat disenchanted with the political process and that they are given so little respect. People's perception is based on fact in some cases, and assumptions in others, and the perception is this: that so often political parties and politicians are not telling people the truth, that they are not necessarily acting in the best interests of the people. We are told half-truths, and these half-truths are spun at us in all sorts of different and wonderful ways. We see no integrity, so we give no trust—and our nation is poorer for the lack of it.

In our Western bubble, this lack of integrity, even though it is causing problems and corruption is growing, has not yet had the devastating impact that can be seen in other nations around the world. But, unfortunately, it is only a matter of time and we can already see, even in our own nation, that the poor and the marginalised have become victims of the lack of integrity.

Integrity doesn't just operate in a political and corporate sense. Integrity is also a value that holds personal relationships together. In our society, we see an unprecedented breakdown in marriage, an equally unprecedented outbreak of violence in relationships, and all manners of abuse, because in simple terms we have no inner integrity.

This could be put another way. Jesus spoke of the fruits of the Spirit: patience, love, kindness and self-control are integrity in action. In other words, we shouldn't just follow our impulses—just because we feel something is right, it doesn't mean it is right; just because I want to do something, it doesn't mean that I should. Integrity asks awkward questions of our actions, our feelings, our desires. It challenges us: 'Is this right?' It is a conscience that is alive; that is not seared with all sorts of compromises.

In our personal relationships, this lack of integrity, this lack of self-control, causes actions and responses that lead our friends and partners to no longer trust us.

In marriage we have promised to love one person and to be faithful. What goes on when no one else can see? Do we have that inner integrity that enables us to resist the temptations that are common to all of us? There is not one person who is not tempted to speak things they should not speak, to do things they should not do, to desire things they should not have because of promises they have made to others. We have common desires and common passions, but integrity—personal integrity—empowers our self-control so that we do not give in to these impulses. It means that we can be trusted.

To be brutally honest, we are currently living in a challenging world because integrity is being divorced from our actions. Our modern culture says to us: 'It doesn't matter if politicians have no integrity in their personal or private lives; we can still trust them. We can still give them high office, because their personal life should not affect their public life.' We are put at ease by this so-called dichotomy, but should we be? If I say one thing and do another in my private life, does that not increase the possibility that I might do the same in my public life?

Jesus said that if we are faithful with the little, we will be faithful with much. Shouldn't we rightly have a certain scepticism that if people are not faithful in one aspect of their lives, that if they do not have integrity in their personal and private lives, it could seep over into all sorts of other areas?

So let's embrace this value of integrity. But here is a warning. It will not be the most comfortable of the values because it will trouble your soul. It will wake you up in the night and question your motives and your actions. But, surely our world would be a better place if more of us were so troubled.

We have looked at four major values and the life values derived from them. Following the thought that transformation begins with a change of our value systems, these values then shape our world which forms our character. But perhaps these values are not just a wonderful transforming idea about discipleship; could they not be an approach for mission as well? What compelling hope does the Christian church offer and could that hope be God's value system? God's presence in these values empowers us to live another way and our world would be a better place and we would be better people if we embrace these values.

On reading through this book you might think there is a value missing and that is to have a high value of planet earth itself. There is no doubt that it was God's intention that we should look after his planet and the church, unfortunately, has not always been at the forefront of the organisations which try and show us what our selfishness and our lack of respect for the planet can do and how it affects everybody.

One strength of today's generation is that they have embraced a high view of the planet. They have welcomed something that is radical and powerful which we also need to acknowledge .

So let us go on a journey together and think about our values and how they can be transformed and the following chapter contains some questions and suggestions that might help you on that journey.

6

Applying the values

Values for work

Most people spend the greatest amount of their time in the place where they work. Jesus called believers to be salt and light in the world (Matthew 5:13 -16). We are to preserve the flavour and to bring the light of God to his world.

What values are particularly relevant to your workplace?

How can a Christian make a difference in the workplace?

How would your colleagues describe you? Would they find you trustworthy, responsible, hard working etc?

Imagine what would happen in your workplace if integrity and honesty were absent. What can you do on a daily basis to encourage these Godly values?

How does a high value of people lead you to treat those around you— your colleagues, your bosses, those who work for you?

In what ways are you valuing the gifts of others?

How are you affected by the need for success at work?

In what ways are you demonstrating faithfulness to do as much as you can with what you have been given?

Values for Marriage

For a marriage to flourish and survive there need to be values that guide the behaviour of both partners. The outworking of these values will provide a foundation for both the wonder of marriage but also the pain of an enduring close relationship.

What values create the foundation for successful marriage?

If you are married, in what ways are you demonstrating that you have a high value of people in your marriage?

How do you treat your partner?
Is there real intimacy—undivided attention, eye focus, real positive listening and question—asking from one partner to another?
How do you convey value?
What expectations do you have?

You could ask your partner 'How do you think that I show that I have a high value of you and our relationship?"

In what ways are you demonstrating a core value of sacrificial love?

When do you do what is right even though you'd like to do what is wrong?
When are you kind rather than being angry?
What sacrifices do you make to live out the relationship in a positive way even when you are emotionally struggling?
In what ways are you giving the gift of forgiveness to your partner?

Values for Mission

Mission is about communicating the essence of the Christian message, through words, actions and love. This message is that there is a God of love who has reached out to us through his son Jesus. Historically we have lived our own way, but through Christ there is a way back to friendship with God. We can be transformed through his love and friendship as our selfishness and sin are dealt with. We in turn become agents of his transforming love to our world.

How do you communicate to people who have a negative view of God and the church? In what ways can we impact a nation that deep in its subconscious holds God responsible for all sorts of ills? How can we change our methods, language and metaphors to keep pace with our changing world? Values can help us to communicate what God is like and how he wants us to live in his kingdom, by giving us a language and a framework which people relate to.

What values do you think form the fabric of our society? Which of these values are Kingdom values?

What does a society look like where there is no love, hope and trust?

We can preach the gospel in terms of love, hope and trust which are recognised by most people as important values holding our society and families together. At the heart of the universe is a God of love who has demonstrated his sacrificial and unconditional love in giving his son Jesus. How would you communicate our message of love, hope and trust to people in your network?

Values for Young People

Being a parent is probably one of the greatest responsibilities any of us is likely to have. It can be the source of some of our happiest and most sublime moments. It will almost certainly be the most heartbreaking, frustrating and challenging experience. As parents, we have the opportunity to influence and guide our children, and to give them a frame of reference for the future. We have a few years to encourage our children to embrace a dynamic value system that will underlie their behaviour.

In our world where there are no 'absolutes', where anything goes—'if it feels right do it'—what absolutes would you want your children to have?

With the strength of peer pressure and cultural norms, what values would you want to shape your children's behaviour whether they are with the family, with other Christians or out with their friends?

If every young person has three driving needs, identity, security and love, how would you want your children to fulfil these needs?

Where would you want your children to get their identity from?

- Their image?
- The people they know?
- Their standing with the opposite sex?
- Their conforming to the behaviour of their peer group?
- Their achievements?
- The love and care of their parents?
- A deep sense of their being children of a loving God who values them?
- A high value of themselves—that they are unique individuals with talents, gifts and potential?

If you want your children to learn about real love, the love which is sacrificial and totally accepting, how will you go about this? What tools will you use to enable your children not to take their value system from their peer group but to catch biblical values which will influence their choices?

In what ways can you pray for your children?

In what ways can you educate your children?

In what ways can you set an authentic example to your children?

How will you set healthy boundaries for your children as they change and grow?

Values for Leadership

There is a crisis in leadership in our modern world. We see it especially in politics, but it is also in the church. Leaders in both these spheres are battling for people's hearts and minds in order to earn the leadership and influence that they have.

Finding a new way to lead does not depend on leadership skills, the ability to think into the future, preaching or teaching skills. These are important but will not cause people to follow. Character and values become the foundation on which the skills of the leader operate. So what are the values of leadership?

What would be the values that you would like to see motivating your leader?

What do you see were the values that motivated Jesus' leadership?

- What was Jesus' attitude to position and power?
- What underpinned Jesus' value of servanthood?
- In what ways did he maximise the potential and possibility of the lives of those he came into contact with?
- What would show that a leader has a high value of relationship?
- People's encounters with Jesus tended to be life changing, physically, emotionally and spiritually. What enabled Jesus to see the potential in people? What value did this demonstrate?

Valuing the Created World

Sometimes I allow myself the joy of contemplating the discussions that might have gone on between the Father, Jesus and the Holy Spirit as they created the world and mankind. As they looked at what they had done, they saw that it was good. How they must have enjoyed that moment!

Loving God surely means loving his creation. How are we to value his creation? Loving others and ourselves has implications for the way we care for the planet. How can we demonstrate that value in the choices we make? We know that in working together to make a difference to our planet we would be honouring God and all he created.

There is no doubt that it was God's intention that we should look after his planet and the church has not always been at the forefront of showing us what our selfishness and lack of respect for the planet can do to damage and abuse what has been given to us. The results of our selfishness are affecting everyone, wherever we live.

If we are to embrace and demonstrate a high view of the planet, we need to be thinking about it. Take a moment now to contemplate our world. You could think of your favourite place on earth or look at some photos on the website. You could look again at a David Attenborough programme that brings the delights into our sitting rooms. Spend time remembering what you know of the latest developments in space exploration or the medical and physical frontiers that are being explored. How about the weather, the range of food and our fellow members of mankind? The list is endless when we think of all that has been and continues to be created.

What today do you most appreciate about God's created world? You could turn that into praise and thanks for all that we have to enjoy which sustains our lives.

Where do you think the greatest abuses of our planet are happening? What are the outcomes of this abuse and what are the implications for our future?

What do you know that is being done, or even talked about, to protect the planet from misuse? Is there anything more that you could be doing to add your weight to the arguments, by being politically aware and active, joining a pressure group or even just becoming more informed and spreading the word?

In what ways are you looking after God's creation in the patch which you inhabit? Are there things that you could do to help maintain its delicate balance?

Cell UK Resources

4Life
by Mark Powley

 As Christians we often struggle to get to grips with key areas of our lives and overcome what seem like ongoing hurdles to our growth and development. If this sounds familiar then read on. Fortunately help is at hand in the form of a discipling booklet called *4Life*. Using four powerful headings of Identity, Values, Lifestyle and Purpose, Mark Powley has written daily thought provoking and challenging material. It is designed to be used by an individual who wants to grow in their relationship with God.

The idea is simple - which is part of its attraction!

There are 10 sessions under each heading and you can do one a day on your own for a couple of weeks or take longer if you like. After each section you meet up with a trusted friend to talk and pray through what you have learnt. The sessions are designed to get you in touch with the underlying issues and include Bible readings, personal stories and relevant facts.

Jennie Bruce, The Gospel Centre, North London adds: '*4Life* is one of the best discipling tools available. It is immensely readable and the author has made it as interactive as possible. We are highly recommending it to people in our church.'

You may be asking 'why is something like this so important now?' There is no doubt that one of the challenges all churches face, is discipleship. In reality this means individuals taking responsibility to follow Jesus and by doing so, being transformed slowly but surely into his likeness.

We have all faced common challenges in this area. The consumerism of the last decade has created an effect where people expect the church to feed them, reducing their personal responsibility. *4Life* puts the responsibility back with the individual, encouraging them to read through the material and respond to the questions on their own and then meet with a mentor to review how they are doing.

We need to recognise that a Christian moral base is no longer inherent in our society so trying to disciple in ways that used to work through teaching imperatives has very limited effect now. Therefore a value based approach is needed that tackles the underlying issues. *4Life* is values based and challenges fundamental areas of life by asking questions that unearth false mind sets and encourage values change.

So take up the challenge and set out on the journey to discover God's values for living by ordering a copy of *4Life* for yourself and a friend to work through together.

Cell UK Resources

Sowing Reaping Keeping
by Laurence Singlehurst

The Christian gospel is the best story ever told. Yet many of those who hear it perceive it as a threat. Laurence Singlehurst believes that much of the threat would be removed if Christians would respect and understand the people they are approaching. This short, crisp and often humorous book is full of seeds of wisdom for those who long to make permanent disciples for Jesus. Discover the reasons why evangelism may have been difficult in the past and learn new ideas to help you share your faith in a relevant way.

Who's Shaping You?
by Graham Cray

This book explains four different foundational issues for us as we set our course to be disciples of Jesus. In doing this Graham gives us an exciting theological vision to help us work out our foundations for living this life. He describes a radical way of life, based on biblical thinking which he sees is necessary if we are to impact our world. He encourages us to allow Jesus to infect the whole of our lives and to live those lives openly in front of those we come across day by day.

For more resources visit our online bookshop
at www.celluk.org.uk

Or phone: 01582 463330
E-mail: cellukresources@oval.com

Payment may be made by credit card or invoice.
Postage and packing will be charged extra.